ULTIMATE AVENGERS

ULTIMATE
AVENGERS

WRITER: PENCILER:

MARK MILLAR   LEINIL FRANCIS YU

INKERS: **GERRY ALANGUILAN**

WITH **JASON PAZ, EDGAR TADEO** & **JEFF HUET**

COLORISTS: **LAURA MARTIN** & **DAVE MCCAIG** WITH **FRANK MARTIN**

LETTERER: **VC'S CORY PETIT**

COVER ART: **LEINIL FRANCIS YU, GERRY ALANGUILAN,**
LAURA MARTIN, DAVE MCCAIG & **MARTE GRACIA**

ASSISTANT EDITOR: **SANA AMANAT**

SENIOR EDITOR: **MARK PANICCIA**

COLLECTION EDITOR: **JENNIFER GRÜNWALD**

EDITORIAL ASSISTANTS: **JAMES EMMETT & JOE HOCHSTEIN**

ASSISTANT EDITORS: **ALEX STARBUCK & NELSON RIBEIRO**

EDITOR, SPECIAL PROJECTS: **MARK D. BEAZLEY**

SENIOR EDITOR, SPECIAL PROJECTS: **JEFF YOUNGQUIST**

SENIOR VICE PRESIDENT OF SALES: **DAVID GABRIEL**

EDITOR IN CHIEF: **JOE QUESADA**   PUBLISHER: **DAN BUCKLEY**

EXECUTIVE PRODUCER: **ALAN FINE**

ULTIMATE COMICS AVENGERS: CRIME AND PUNISHMENT. Contains material originally published in magazine form as ULTIMATE AVENGERS 2 #1-6. First printing 2010. Hardcover ISBN# 978-0-7851-3670-5. Softcover ISBN# 978-0-7851-3671-2. Published by MARVEL WORLDWIDE, INC., a subsidiary of MARVEL ENTERTAINMENT, LLC. OFFICE OF PUBLICATION: 417 5th Avenue, New York, NY 10016. Copyright © 2010 and 2011 Marvel Characters, Inc. All rights reserved. Hardcover: $24.99 per copy in the U.S. and $27.99 in Canada (GST #R127032852). $19.99 per copy in the U.S. and $22.50 in Canada (GST #R127032852). Canadian Agreement #40668537. All characters featured in this issue and the distinctive names and likenesses thereof, and all related indicia are trademarks of Marvel Characters, Inc. No similarity between any of the names, characters, persons, and/or institutions in this magazine with those of any living or dead person or institution is intended, and any such similarity which may exist is purely coincidental. **Printed in the U.S.A.** ALAN FINE, EVP - Office of the President, Marvel Worldwide, Inc. and EVP & CMO Marvel Characters B.V.; DAN BUCKLEY, Chief Executive Officer and Publisher - Print, Animation & Digital Media; JIM SOKOLOWSKI, Chief Operating Officer; DAVID GABRIEL, SVP of Publishing Sales & Circulation; DAVID BOGART, SVP of Business Affairs & Talent Management; MICHAEL PASCIULLO, VP Merchandising & Communications; JIM O'KEEFE, VP of Operations & Logistics; DAN CARR, Executive Director of Publishing Technology; JUSTIN F. GABRIE, Director of Publishing & Editorial Operations; SUSAN CRESPI, Editorial Operations Manager; ALEX MORALES, Publishing Operations Manager; STAN LEE, Chairman Emeritus. For information regarding advertising in Marvel Comics or on Marvel.com, please contact Ron Stern, VP of Business Development, at rstern@marvel.com. For Marvel subscription inquiries, please call 800-217-9158. **Manufactured between** 9/6/10 and 10/6/10 (hardcover), and 9/6/10 and 3/23/11 (softcover), by R.R. DONNELLEY, INC., SALEM, VA, USA.

10 9 8 7 6 5 4 3 2 1

1

THE PUNISHER
GETS BUSY:

BLAM!

BLAM!

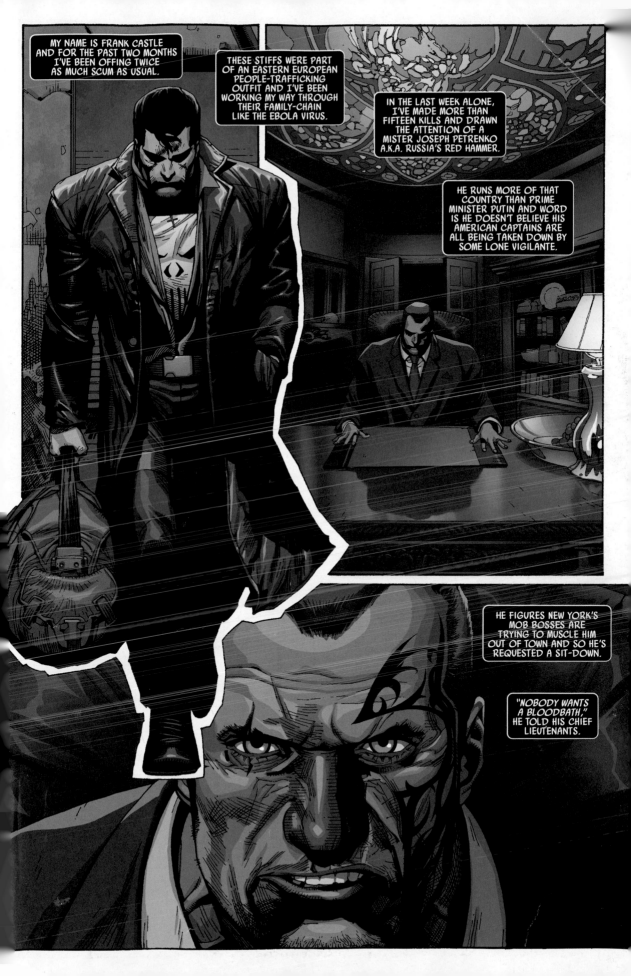

MY NAME IS FRANK CASTLE AND FOR THE PAST TWO MONTHS I'VE BEEN OFFING TWICE AS MUCH SCUM AS USUAL.

THESE STIFFS WERE PART OF AN EASTERN EUROPEAN PEOPLE-TRAFFICKING OUTFIT AND I'VE BEEN WORKING MY WAY THROUGH THEIR FAMILY-CHAIN LIKE THE EBOLA VIRUS.

IN THE LAST WEEK ALONE, I'VE MADE MORE THAN FIFTEEN KILLS AND DRAWN THE ATTENTION OF A MISTER JOSEPH PETRENKO A.K.A. RUSSIA'S RED HAMMER.

HE RUNS MORE OF THAT COUNTRY THAN PRIME MINISTER PUTIN AND WORD IS HE DOESN'T BELIEVE HIS AMERICAN CAPTAINS ARE ALL BEING TAKEN DOWN BY SOME LONE VIGILANTE.

HE FIGURES NEW YORK'S MOB BOSSES ARE TRYING TO MUSCLE HIM OUT OF TOWN AND SO HE'S REQUESTED A SIT-DOWN.

"NOBODY WANTS A BLOODBATH," HE TOLD HIS CHIEF LIEUTENANTS.

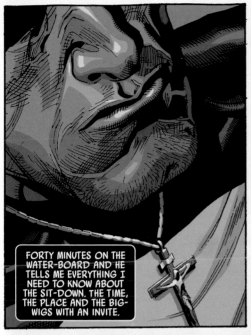

FORTY MINUTES ON THE WATER-BOARD AND HE TELLS ME EVERYTHING I NEED TO KNOW ABOUT THE SIT-DOWN. THE TIME, THE PLACE AND THE BIG-WIGS WITH AN INVITE.

I SAY THANKS AND SEND HIM FOR A SWIM.

LEXINGTON AVENUE:

THE CHEAPEST ROOMS AT THIS HOTEL ARE A THOUSAND BUCKS A NIGHT. BUT THE RED HAMMER DOESN'T STAY IN A ROOM. HE STAYS IN A *SUITE* AND THEY START AT *FIVE GRAND*--

--ALL PAID FOR BY THOSE LITTLE GIRLS WORKING EIGHTEEN HOUR DAYS IN HIS FLEA-PITS ACROSS TOWN.

Astoria Pla

THEIR SIT-DOWN'S HAPPENING AN HOUR FROM NOW. PLENTY OF TIME TO GRAB SOME OF THAT AMERICAN FOOD HE'S TAKEN SUCH A LIKING TO...

I WANT BURGER, BUT NOT BURGER KING. I LIKE MCDONALD'S. YOU UNDERSTAND?

QUITE A *PREDICAMENT* YOU GOT YOURSELF IN, FRANK. HOW DOES A NICE BOY LIKE YOU END UP BECOMING AMERICA'S MOST NOTORIOUS *MULTIPLE KILLER?*

IT SAYS HERE YOU USED TO BE AN *ALTAR BOY.*

WHAT HAPPENED TO THE RED HAMMER?

EXTRADITED BACK TO RUSSIA.

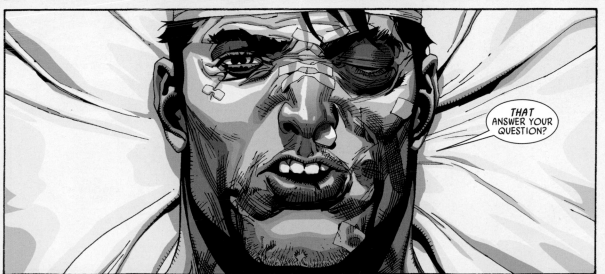

THAT ANSWER YOUR QUESTION?

WHICH ALL SOUNDS PRETTY COOL: HONEST COP'S FAMILY TAKEN DOWN BY THE MOB SO HONEST COP TAKES THE WAR TO *THE BAD GUYS*...

...EXCEPT SOME OF YOUR VICTIMS AIN'T EXACTLY AL CAPONE. WE'RE TALKING DRIVERS, BAG-MEN, EVEN *KIDS* SOMETIMES.

THAT BOY BACK IN CHELSEA HEIGHTS WAS IN HIGH SCHOOL, FRANK...

NOW MY QUERY IS...

...HOW DO WE KEEP A USEFUL GUY LIKE YOU OFFA *DEATH ROW?*

WHAT DO YOU *WANT* FROM ME?

I LIKE HIM. HE'S SMART.

DO YOU KNOW WHO I AM, FRANK?

OF COURSE I KNOW WHO YOU ARE. YOU'RE NICK FURY. YOU USED TO RUN THE ULTIMATES.

WELL, NOT ANYMORE. ONCE UPON A TIME, I PISSED SOME PEOPLE OFF SO NOW I RUN S.H.I.E.L.D.'S BLACK OPS DIVISION WITH CODENAME BLACK WIDOW HERE.

THE REST OF THE AVENGERS ARE CURRENTLY BEING ASSEMBLED. YOU CAN MEET THEM AT EIGHTEEN HUNDRED HOURS.

WE GET PAID TO DO THE DIRTY STUFF. THE KINDA JOBS CAPTAIN AMERICA AND HIS FRIENDS WOULD BALK AT...

...HENCE THE REASON WE'RE AFTER A CAPTAIN AMERICA OF OUR OWN.

"...THE FIRST HULK."

2

SOUTH AMERICA:

SO *TELL* ME, DOCTOR BANNER...

...WHY DO YOU *REALLY* WANT TO JOIN MY TEAM?

TO *LEARN,* OF COURSE. TO BE A PART OF SOMETHING THAT COULD CHANGE THE WORLD *FOREVER.*

MY OWN COUNTRY ISN'T INTERESTED IN SUPER-SOLDIERS ANYMORE AND YOU PEOPLE ARE.

IT'S THAT *SIMPLE.*

BUT WHY *THIS* PROJECT? WHAT DRAWS YOU TO THE IDEA OF TAKING AN ORDINARY LITTLE MAN AND TURNING HIM INTO THE *PERFECT HUMAN SPECIMEN?*

BE *HONEST* WITH YOURSELF.

SO?

WE KNOW WHO YOU *ARE*, SIR. WE KNOW ABOUT THE MURDER AND THE VIOLENCE YOU'VE BEEN HOOKED ON SINCE YOU TURNED YOUR BACK ON YOUR OLD LIFE.

WE KNOW YOU PRACTICALLY *RUN* THIS PLACE SINCE YOU OFFED THE LOCAL GANGLORDS.

THOSE ARE *THEIR* CARS YOU'RE DRIVING BACK THERE. *THEIR* GIRLFRIENDS YOU BEEN SLEEPING WITH.

MY NAME IS *TYRONE CASH*.

I'M A *BUSINESSMAN*.

NO, YOUR NAME IS *LEONARD WILLIAMS* AND YOU'RE THE GENIUS WHO TAUGHT BRUCE BANNER EVERYTHING HE KNOWS.

NOW COME BACK HOME BEFORE THINGS GET OUT OF HAND...

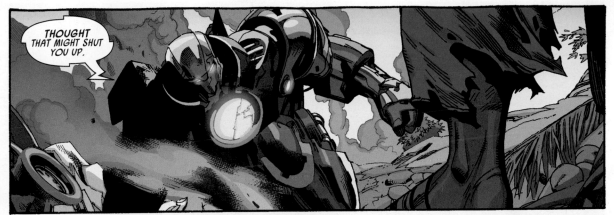

S.H.I.E.L.D. OUTPOST, NEW JERSEY:

GENERAL FURY GATHERS HIS HIT-MEN:

WOW. NICE DIGS, NICK. I ALWAYS *FELT* THE TRISKELION WAS MISSING THAT PUTRID STENCH OF *URINE.*

THIS ISN'T THE *ULTIMATES*, HAWKEYE. IT'S A *DEATH SQUAD.* *LOW-KEY* IS THE NAME OF THE GAME.

SO WHAT AM I DOING IN THIS *STUPID COSTUME?*

BECAUSE IT'S *BULLETPROOF*, MISTER CASTLE, AND AS LONG AS YOU'RE WEARING IT NOBODY KNOWS WE'RE FRATERNIZING WITH *THE PUNISHER.*

I DON'T KNOW WHAT YOU'RE BITCHING ABOUT ANYWAY. YOU STILL GET TO *SHOOT GUNS* AND KILL GUYS.

DON'T PATRONIZE ME, RHODES. I'M NOT IN THE MOOD.

JUST SAY THE WORD, FRANK. I CAN SEND YOU BACK TO DEATH ROW ANYTIME YOU LIKE.

LOOK, COULD WE JUST GET ON WITH THIS $@% MEETING? I'M LOSING A *FORTUNE* BEING HERE.

CASH IS RIGHT. EVEN I HAVEN'T HEARD WHO WE'RE SUPPOSED TO BE TAKING OUT.

THAT'S BECAUSE WE'RE STILL NOT SURE *OURSELVES*, HAWKEYE. ALL I KNOW IS THAT THE ORDER CAME STRAIGHT FROM THE *WHITE HOUSE...*

"...AND IT SCARES THE *LIVING HELL* OUTTA ME."

3

"BUT THE WEIRDEST MURDER WAS OIL MAGNATE *NELSON FORD*. WHAT HAPPENED TO HIM WE'RE NOT EVEN *SURE...*"

PETRIFIED

ROASTED

WHO HE'S WORKING FOR IS A *TOTAL MYSTERY*. *WHAT* HE IS WE HAVE NO IDEA.

ALL WE KNOW IS THAT HE'S SEVEN FEET TALL, AS STRONG AS THOR AND PROBABLY SOME KIND OF *GENETIC MUTATION*.

JESUS.

WHAT ELSE LINKS THE VICTIMS BESIDES BEING *RICH?*

THAT'S FOR YOU TO *FIND OUT,* HAWKEYE.

ISN'T THIS SOMETHING THAT *DAYTIME* TEAM COULD BE DOING? HOW COME *THE ULTIMATES* AREN'T ALL OVER THIS?

BECAUSE THIS ISN'T A *RESCUE MISSION,* RHODEY. THIS ISN'T SOME *SUPER VILLAIN* WE WANT TOSSED IN JAIL.

WORD FROM ABOVE IS THE *MUTIE DIES.* THIS IS AN *EXECUTION ORDER.*

FORGET ABOUT IT. WHY SHOULD I PROTECT THE GOVERNMENT'S *RICH FRIENDS?* THESE PUNKS PROBABLY JUST GOT WHAT THEY *DESERVED.*

YOU DON'T UNDERSTAND, MISTER CASTLE. PROJECT AVENGERS ISN'T McDONALDS.

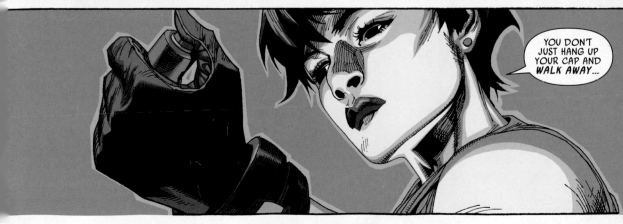

YOU DON'T JUST HANG UP YOUR CAP AND *WALK AWAY...*

AAAGH!

WHAT THE HELL WAS *THAT*, WIDOW?

NEURAL-IMPLANT HIDDEN DEEP INSIDE YOUR HEAD. ALL PART OF YOUR *REHABILITATION PROCESS.*

ARE YOU OUT OF YOUR *MIND?*

$#*#%!

NEVER POINT A GUN AT A TEAM-MATE, FRANK. BAD MANNERS.

I GOTTA ADMIT, I DIDN'T WANT TO BE HERE, BUT THIS IS PRETTY ENTERTAINING.

SHUT UP, CASH.

THE ESTATE OF NELSON FORD, SAN FRANCISCO:

WHAT YOU THINK OF THAT BLACK WIDOW BIRD? I RECKON SHE'S A *RIGHT* LITTLE MINX. I WONDER WHY SHE AND FURY BROKE UP. YOU THINK SHE MIGHT HAVE BEEN *TOO DIRTY* FOR HIM?

I THINK I'M *TOO SCARED* TO EVEN *HAVE* THIS CONVERSATION.

I THINK SHE'D LIKE A LITTLE *SPANKING* FROM THE BIG MAN, MATE. YOU NOTICE HOW I DIDN'T GET ONE OF HER STUPID *IMPLANTS?*

THAT'S BECAUSE WE'VE GOT *OTHER* WAYS OF CONTROLLING YOU, TYRONE...

...PLUS NOBODY COULD FIND A DRILL *HARD* ENOUGH.

YOU *BELIEVE* THIS? IT'S LIKE SOMETHING OUT OF *THE OLD TESTAMENT.*

WHAT ARE YOU TALKING ABOUT?

ALL THESE MASHED UP BODIES. THIS GUY TURNED TO *STONE.* ISN'T THAT WHAT HAPPENED TO *LOT'S* WIFE IN THE *BIBLE?*

LOT'S WIFE WAS TURNED INTO *SALT,* BUDDY. NOW STOP TRYING TO SOUND CLEVER AND JUST TELL US WHAT INTEL CAME UP WITH.

THEIR FILES HAVE BEEN CHECKED AND TRIPLE-CHECKED, SIR. ONLY THING WE FOUND IS THAT ALL FOUR TARGETS WERE IN THE WHITE HOUSE BIKER CORPS.

THE WHAT?

AN EXCLUSIVE CLUB WHERE RICH GUYS MEET UP ONCE A YEAR FOR A *CHARITY BIKE RIDE.*

IT'S A LONG SHOT, I KNOW, BUT WE'RE SENDING AGENTS TO COVER ALL THE OTHER MEMBERS. JUST TO BE ON THE SAFE SIDE.

WHAT ABOUT *THIS* GUY? WHO'S HE?

OH, THAT'S JUST THE HOUSEKEEPER. THE DECEASED'S *PERSONAL ASSISTANT.* NOBODY KNOWS WHY, BUT HE'S THE ONE GUY WHO *SURVIVED* LAST NIGHT...

ODD.

WHAT'S SO SPECIAL ABOUT HIM?

CHICAGO O'HARE AIRPORT:

CHRIST IN PAIN, BRUTAL CHARACTER ASSASSINATION. NINE LETTERS.

HMMM...

4

YOU GOING FOR A JUMP, PUNISHER?

JUST TRYING TO BUILD UP A LITTLE *SPEED*, HAWKEYE.

BLACK WIDOW HIT A HUNDRED AND TEN IN HER STARK-SUIT--

GOOD NIGHT, SWEET PRINCE.

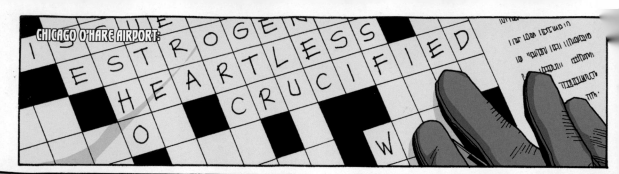

HEH.

OF COURSE.

HELLO THERE.

WOULD YOU LIKE TO READ THE *FUNNIES?*

THE TRISKELION, NEW YORK. HEADQUARTERS OF THE ULTIMATES:

ARE YOU KIDDING ME? BLACK OPS IS MOVING IN AGAIN?

ORDERS FROM THE WHITE HOUSE, COLONEL DANVERS. OBVIOUSLY, I DON'T WANT TO TREAD ON ANYONE'S TOES, BUT THIS GHOST RIDER SITUATION IS NOW A *PRESIDENTIAL PRIORITY.*

SO WHY WASN'T I INFORMED?

BECAUSE THIS IS STILL THREE LEVELS ABOVE TOP SECRET, CAROL. NEITHER YOU NOR YOUR ULTIMATES ARE REQUIRED IN THIS OPERATION.

YOU'RE LOVING THIS, AREN'T YOU, FURY?

OH, YEAH.

NOW WE STILL DON'T HAVE ANYTHING *CONCRETE* ON THIS FREAK, BUT CODENAME NERD HULK INFORMS ME THAT *THE SPIDER* HAS SOME *PSYCHIC INTEL.*

BLACK WIDOW IS DOWNSTAIRS WITH THEM NOW TRYING TO FIGURE OUT WHAT WE CAN *USE.*

I DIDN'T KNOW THE SPIDER WAS *PSYCHIC.*

OF *COURSE* HE'S PSYCHIC, HE'S THE LOVE-CHILD OF SPIDER-MAN AND CHARLES XAVIER, BACK FROM THE FUTURE WITH A WARNING FOR HUMANITY.

SERIOUSLY?

UNBELIEVABLE.

SHE REALLY IS AS STUPID AS YOU *SAID* SHE WAS, NICK.

WELL. AT LEAST NOW I KNOW WHERE ALL MY CONTRACTS HAVE BEEN GOING.

OH, FOR GOD'S SAKE, TONY. WHAT ARE YOU TALKING ABOUT? GREGORY'S ALWAYS HANDLED BLACK OPS.

JUST IGNORE HIM, GENERAL.

HE'S A BEEN LITTL

HALF A MILE BELOW:

INFORMATION ON THE GHOST RIDER REQUIRES A *FORFEIT*, NERD HULK.

ACTUALLY, WE'VE DECIDED ON *BANNER*. NERD HULK IS PRETTY DEMEANING FOR SOMEONE WHO'S BEEN MADE AN OFFICIAL MEMBER OF *STAFF*.

OH, I THINK NERD HULK IS A *WAY* BETTER NAME FOR A BILLION-DOLLAR CLONE THAT DOESN'T KNOW HOW TO FIGHT.

THEY GAVE YOU THIS JOB FOR SOMETHING TO *DO*, FAT-ASS. I HEAR THEM MAKING JOKES ABOUT YOU THAT WOULD HAVE YOU ON YOUR *KNEES*.

SOMETHING SAD AND PAINFUL I MIGHT FIND FUNNY. LIKE YOUR SEPARATION FROM GENERAL FURY, BLACK WIDOW. WHAT MADE TWO LITTLE LOVEBIRDS GO THEIR SEPARATE WAYS?

HE SAW THIS IN A MOVIE ONCE AND THOUGHT IT LOOKED *COOL*. I CAN LEAVE IF IT MAKES YOU UNCOMFORTABLE.

HE DOESN'T SPOOK ME.

I NEVER FOUND IT EASY TO MAKE FRIENDS, BUT I WAS ALWAYS CLOSE WITH MY MOTHER AND SISTERS. NIGHTS OUT WITH THEM WERE THE ONLY TIMES I EVER REALLY *LAUGHED*.

"THEY ALL LOVED NICK, OF COURSE. ESPECIALLY AFTER HE SAVED ME FROM THAT BAD SCENE IN BOSNIA.

"THEY WERE PLEASED TO SEE ME SETTLE DOWN AND THE FIRST FEW MONTHS WERE ALL THE USUAL FAIRYTALE STUFF.

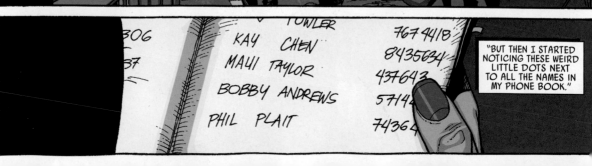

TOWLER 767 4418
306
KAY CHEN 8435634
37
MAUI TAYLOR 437643
BOBBY ANDREWS 5714
PHIL PLAIT 74364

"BUT THEN I STARTED NOTICING THESE WEIRD LITTLE DOTS NEXT TO ALL THE NAMES IN MY PHONE BOOK."

"IT WOULDN'T REGISTER WITH MOST PEOPLE, BUT I'VE BEEN TRAINED TO SPOT THE SMALLEST DETAILS. EVERY TIME I WENT OFF ON A MISSION I'D COME BACK HOME TO FIND MORE LITTLE DOTS.

"BESIDE MY MOM. BESIDE MY SISTERS. BESIDE MY *COUSINS...*

OH DEAR.

IN A FEW SHORT MONTHS HE'D SLEPT WITH EVERY WOMAN IN MY FAMILY AND WHAT FEW FRIENDS I HAD.

MM. AND YET YOU'RE STILL IN LOVE WITH HIM, DEEP DOWN.

WHY?

HE'S *NICK FURY.*

WHO *WOULDN'T* BE IN LOVE WITH HIM?

POOR LITTLE MONICA.

MY TURN NOW...

"TWENTY YEARS AGO, THE GHOST RIDER WAS CALLED JOHNNY BLAZE AND HE AND HIS GIRLFRIEND ROXANNE WERE DOING THIS BIG COAST-TO-COAST ROAD TRIP.

"THEY'D JUST GOT ENGAGED IN TUCSON, ARIZONA, AND WERE OUT CELEBRATING WITH THE FIFTEEN DOLLARS AND TWENTY-EIGHT CENTS THEY STILL HAD BETWEEN THEM.

"THE BIKERS THEY MET THAT NIGHT WERE SUPER-FRIENDLY, ESPECIALLY BOBBY BLACKTHORNE. HE BOUGHT THE COUPLE FREEZING COLD BEERS ALL NIGHT LONG--

"IT WAS ONLY AFTER CLOSING THEY FOUND OUT THE PRICE.

"THE COPS CALLED THE MURDER A *RITUAL KILLING*, JOHNNY BLAZE FOUND WITH HIS THROAT SLIT WIDE AND EVERY DROP OF BLOOD DRAINED FROM HIS BODY.

"BOBBY BLACKTHORNE AND HIS FRIENDS WENT ON TO BECOME SOME OF THE RICHEST MEN IN AMERICA AND THOSE IN THE KNOW BELIEVE IT WAS ALL DOWN TO THE SACRIFICE...

"...AN OFFERING TO SATAN FOR THE LIVES THEY DREAMED OF."

THESE ARE THE RICH GUYS YOU'VE BEEN FINDING IN BITS AND PIECES, MONICA. BECAUSE JOHNNY BLAZE IS BACK AND HE'S HANDING THEM *THEIR ASSES.*

WHAT ARE YOU TALKING ABOUT?

"SATAN OFFERED HIM A DEAL *TOO*, YOU SEE. DOUBLE-CROSSING HIS DISCIPLES AND OFFERING JOHNNY A CHANCE FOR *REVENGE.*

"BUT REVENGE WASN'T ENOUGH..."

HE HAD TO MAKE SURE ROXANNE WAS OKAY AND SO HE SOLD HIS SOUL TO SPARE HER LIFE. NOW SHE'S LIVING IN *ILLINOIS* SOMEWHERE.

"HUSBAND, KIDS, WORKING IN AN OFFICE AND SEX TWICE A WEEK.

"*BLAZE* ON THE OTHER HAND...

"THEY SPENT *TWENTY YEARS* PREPARING HIM FOR THIS.

"WASHING AWAY HIS CHRISTIAN BAPTISM. BURNING ANYTHING SOFT INSIDE.

"BUT NOW HE'S BACK...

"...TO DO *SATAN'S* WORK..."

MISS ABRAHAMS, I WANT YOU TO CONTACT GENERAL FURY AND TELL HIM I WANT MY S.H.I.E.L.D. GUARD *DOUBLED* TONIGHT.

ABSOLUTELY, SIR.

ARE YOU SAYING THE GHOST RIDER HAS A *SUPERNATURAL* EXPLANATION? THAT'S THE MOST *RETARDED* THING I EVER HEARD.

YOU *THINK?*

"ONLY TWO WERE STILL ALIVE FROM THAT OLD *BIKER GANG* AND ONE OF THEM JUST OPENED HIS *WRISTS*, NERD HULK.

"HE KNEW WHAT WAS COMING AND JUST COULDN'T *FACE* IT.

I'M WORKING LATE IN MY OFFICE, SERGEANT, AND I DON'T WANT TO BE DISTURBED.

YES, SIR.

THE LAST ONE ALIVE IS THE *LEADER* OF THE CREW. MAN, DID HE DO WELL FOR HIMSELF: POWER, MONEY, INTERNATIONAL RECOGNITION...

WHAT ARE YOU *SAYING*, SPIDER?

OH, MONICA. YOU DISAPPOINT ME.

"WHO DO YOU THINK PASSED DOWN THAT *EXECUTION ORDER?* THAT MEMO CAME STRAIGHT FROM *THE WHITE HOUSE,* SWEETHEART..."

5

LOOK AT THEM. THEY THINK HE'S A *MUTANT*, DON'T THEY? IF ONLY THEY KNEW WHAT THEY'RE UP AGAINST, BLACKTHORNE.

HE'LL CUT THROUGH THEM LIKE A KNIFE THROUGH *BUTTER*.

THAT'S WHY I NEED *YOUR* HELP, MASTER. YOU MADE ME THE VICE-PRESIDENT. I CAN'T LOSE IT ALL TO THIS IDIOT *JOHNNY BLAZE*...

YOU KNOW MY PRICE, OF COURSE. ARE YOU *REALLY* READY TO GIVE UP THAT WHICH IS MOST SACRED AND PERSONAL?

WHAT ARE YOU TALKING ABOUT? MY SOUL'S ALREADY *DAMNED*. WE SLIT A MAN'S *THROAT* AND DRANK HIS *BLOOD*...

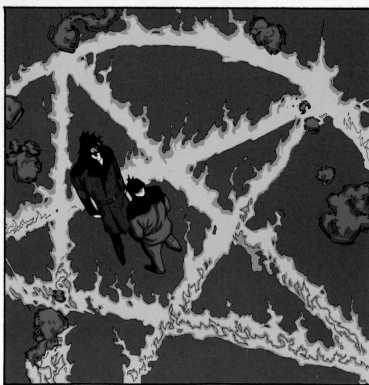
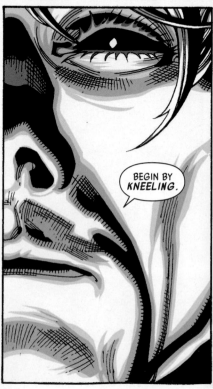

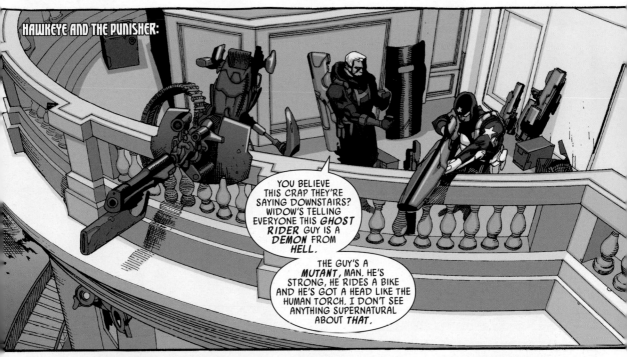

YOU BELIEVE THIS CRAP THEY'RE SAYING DOWNSTAIRS? WIDOW'S TELLING EVERYONE THIS *GHOST RIDER* GUY IS A *DEMON* FROM *HELL*.

THE GUY'S A *MUTANT*, MAN. HE'S STRONG, HE RIDES A BIKE AND HE'S GOT A HEAD LIKE THE HUMAN TORCH. I DON'T SEE ANYTHING SUPERNATURAL ABOUT *THAT*.

I THOUGHT YOU WERE SUPPOSED TO BE *CHRISTIAN*, HAWKEYE. ISN'T THAT *BASED* ON THE IDEA OF AN AFTERLIFE?

OH, YEAH. I FORGOT. HE PASSED YOU A *MESSAGE*, DIDN'T HE? SO WHAT DID HE SAY THAT WAS SO DAMN *CONVINCING?*

SOMETHING THAT WARMED MY HEART.

THAT'S ALL YOU NEED TO KNOW.

"JOHNNY BLAZE IS OUTSIDE NOW. BLUE, DEAD FINGERS TOUCHING COLD STEEL RAILINGS..."

"...HE CAN *SMELL* YOU IN HERE, BLACKTHORNE. I FEEL HIS HEART CATCHING FIRE AS HE STARTS TO *TRANSFORM*."

WHY DID YOU DO IT, MASTER? WHY DID YOU GIVE BLAZE THIS *OPPORTUNITY?*

BECAUSE HE SOLD ME HIS SOUL... AND IN BRINGING HIM BACK I GET YOUR SOUL TOO. YOU AND ALL THOSE *OTHER* FOOLS HE'S BEEN SENDING ME LATELY.

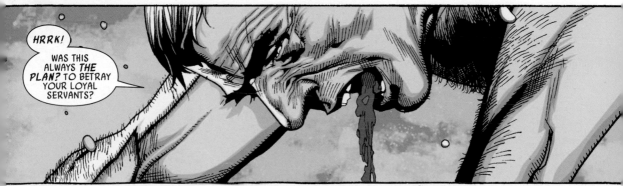

HRRK!

WAS THIS ALWAYS *THE PLAN?* TO BETRAY YOUR LOYAL SERVANTS?

WHAT HAPPENED TO *CASH*, RHODEY? I THOUGHT HE WAS TRAVELLING WITH YOU.

I THINK HE HITCHED A RIDE IN A *HUMMER* OR SOMETHING. SAID HE'D LOOK LIKE A *BITCH* IF HE WAS FLYING IN MY ARMS LIKE LOIS LANE.

I WISH YOU'D STOP CALLING HIM *AFRICAN-AMERICAN,* BY THE WAY. IT'S OKAY TO SAY "BLACK" IF HE'S *ENGLISH.* I WON'T THINK YOU'RE *RACIST.*

I DUNNO, I JUST FEEL A LITTLE *AWKWARD* ABOUT IT. DO YOU THINK THE CORRECT TERM MIGHT BE *AFRICAN-ENGLISH?*

OH, FOR GOD'S SAKE. WE'RE TALKING ABOUT A MAN WHO LITERALLY MADE *FURNITURE* OUT OF HIS *GANGLAND RIVALS.*

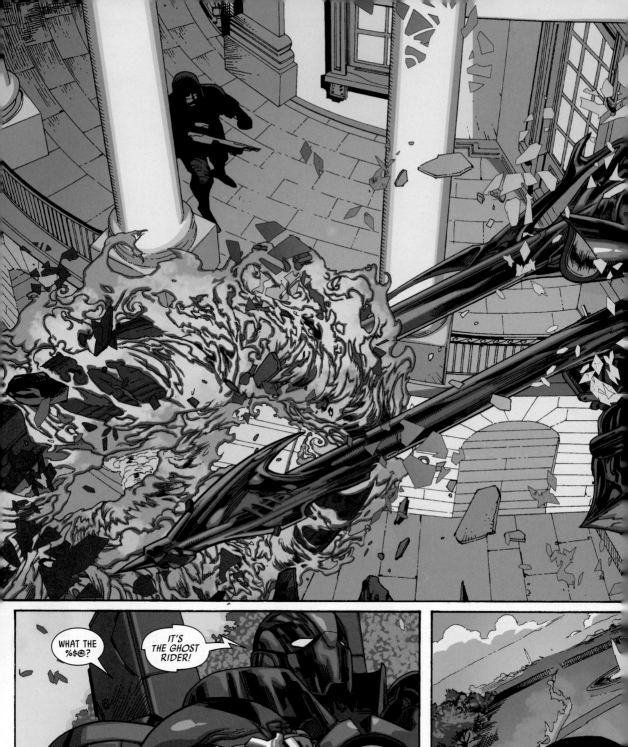

WHAT THE %$@?

IT'S THE GHOST RIDER!

PUNISHER, FORM A TEAM AND GET AFTER HIM!

I'LL GO CHECK ON THE VP!

THE TRISKELION:

RHODEY, THIS IS NICK. I WANT YOU TO HIT HIM WITH EVERYTHING GREG PACKED. YOU HEAR ME? TAKE THIS MOTHER *DOWN!*

I CAN'T WITHOUT HITTING *CIVILIANS!* HE'S WEAVING IN AND OUT OF *TRAFFIC!*

GET *AWAY* FROM ME, RHODES--

THIS HAS BEEN COMING FOR *TWENTY YEARS*, BLACKTHORNE...

Leini
Gerry A.

HUH?

TAKE HIM DOWN!

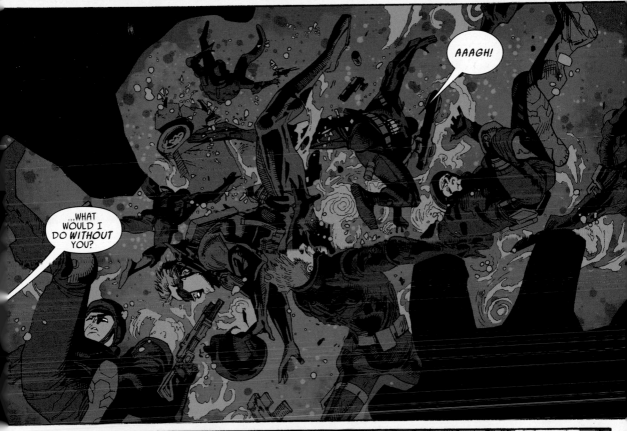

WHAT HAPPENED TO THE *GHOST RIDER?*

I LET HIM GO.

WHAT?

WHY SHOULD HE DIE FOR KILLING *SCUM?* I LET HIM GO BECAUSE JOHNNY BLAZE WAS OFFING ALL THE RIGHT PEOPLE, HAWKEYE.

WILL YOU DO THE SAME FOR *ME?*

ARE YOU OUT OF YOUR MIND?

I NEVER HURT ANYONE WHO DIDN'T *DESERVE* IT. NEVER ONCE TOOK AN *INNOCENT* LIFE. I JUST KILL *VERMIN.* THE KINDA TRASH THAT DESTROYS PEOPLE'S *LIVES.*

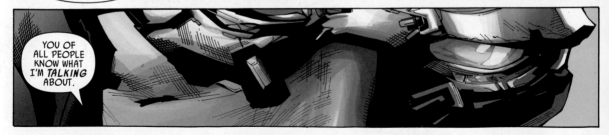

YOU OF ALL PEOPLE KNOW WHAT I'M *TALKING* ABOUT.

WHERE DID THEY PUT MY *IMPLANT*, CLINT? PLEASE! SHOW ME *WHERE* AND I CAN CUT IT *OUT!*

HAWKEYE! PUNISHER! STAY WHERE YOU ARE AND *AWAIT* S.H.I.E.L.D. PICK-UP!

DON'T *HAND* ME IN, SOLDIER! THIS IS MY *LAST CHANCE!* HELP ME OUT SO I CAN DO WHAT *I DO BEST!*

I CAN'T BELIEVE YOU WERE GOOD FOR YOUR WORD. BUT HERE SHE IS JUST LIVING HER LIFE. DO YOU REALLY HAVE THE POWER TO DO THIS?

I CAN DO ANYTHING, JOHNNY BLAZE. WALK ON WATER, HEAL THE SICK...

"...EVEN RAISE THE DEAD."

DOES SHE REMEMBER THE MURDER?

ROXANNE SIMPSON REMEMBERS NOTHING. I THOUGHT IT BEST FOR EVERYONE CONCERNED.

SHE'S MARRIED TO A FIREFIGHTER NOW, BY THE WAY. I'M TOLD THEY HAVE A VERY SATISFYING SEX LIFE.

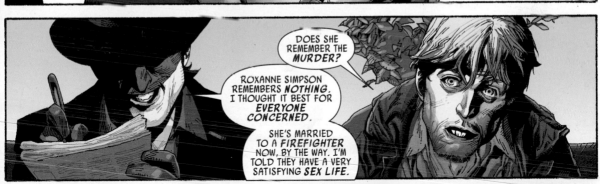

I'M HAPPY FOR HER. I DON'T CARE WHAT HAPPENS TO ME. THE NIGHT SHE DIED WAS ALL MY FAULT. I'M JUST PLEASED I WAS ABLE TO FIX THINGS.

AT A PRICE, OF COURSE.

THIRD MOLAR FROM THE BACK. DON'T PRETEND YOU DIDN'T KNOW.

THAT'S A HELL OF AN *ACCUSATION*, GENERAL.

DON'T *MESS* WITH ME, SON. HAWKEYE DOESN'T MISS A *TARGET*.

JUST MAKE SURE THIS ISN'T YOUR *OLD, REBELLIOUS SELF* MAKING A LITTLE COMEBACK HERE...

...I GOT A *MILLION* OF THOSE IMPLANTS BACK AT BASE.

FROM THE JOURNAL OF FRANK CASTLE:

GETTING OUT OF THE COUNTRY FOR A WHILE SEEMED LIKE A SMART IDEA.

RUSSIA MADE THE MOST SENSE GIVEN RED HAMMER'S *EXTRADITION ORDER.*

IT TOOK ME *TWO DAYS* AND *EIGHT HUNDRED BULLETS* TO FIND THE OLD STEEL MILL WHERE SOME CROOKED COPS HAD BEEN *HIDING* THIS PUNK.

BUT I DIDN'T MIND THE *COLD.* I DIDN'T MIND THE *DAMP.* I DIDN'T EVEN MIND THE *STOMACH WOUND* ONE OF HIS HOOKERS GAVE ME WHEN I TRIED TO *HELP.*

THAT MESSAGE FROM THE OTHER SIDE WARMED ME UP LIKE A *BILLION-WATT BULB.*

BUT WHO DID IT COME FROM? MY *WIFE?* MY *KIDS?* A BLESSING FROM MY *PARENTS?*